De-Stress
Your Holidays

By Jennifer L. Rowe, LCSW

How to Holiday Shop and Remain Stress-Free

De-Stress Your Holidays

HOW TO HOLIDAY SHOP AND REMAIN STRESS-FREE

Gratitude: I want to thank my friend Nicole A. for asking me to write a booklet about how I shop for the holidays. Nicole likes the creativity of the gifts I give and how relaxed I am in December. It took me a few years, but here it is.

I also want to thank my love, Mike, who is a constant guiding light on my life journey. He also shakes his head, rolls his eyes, and dramatically sighs (followed by an amused smile) at how my brain works as I focus on gift-giving year-round.

I am grateful to Amy W. for her advice, which served as the catalyst for me to finally make the changes I needed to. We all need an Amy in our lives. Amy was the kind of friend who told you what you needed to do directly to your face and with the most incredible amount of love as she delivered advice. Even though Amy passed earlier this year, I hear her voice and feel her presence sagely guiding me, and I miss her every day.

I want to thank my sons, Johnathan and Jason, who were the strongest inspirations for this booklet. They are why I changed how I shopped and reduced my holiday stress. I wanted them to have a calmer mother and enjoy making their holiday memories.

With gratitude,
Jennifer Rowe, LCSW
Owner of Journey Life Balance, Inc

AI was not used to generate any of the content in this booklet.

Table of Contents

Welcome to Destress Your Holidays.

I am Jennifer Rowe, a licensed clinical social worker and certified mindset coach who helps others cultivate purpose and meaning in their lives.

I am also an organized holiday shopper and creative gift buyer who has developed tools and a year-round system to make my holidays stress-free. Although I celebrate Christmas, my intent is to share strategies that can be applied to any holiday or annual gift-giving event.

My Story

Picture this—the holidays starring a single mom financially struggling to make ends meet. Sprinkle in a ridiculous amount of holiday stress stirred with perfectionistic expectations to create the perfect recipe for an annual disaster.

Many of us put pressure on ourselves to make perfect holidays. When my boys were younger, I put tremendous stress on myself to give them, now young adults, the best holiday season and memories.

I went all out! I decorated the house top to bottom and spent a ridiculous amount of money trying to make the "perfect holiday" for my boys. In truth, I was stressing my kids out because I was resentful when they did not want to help me, did not enjoy all I did for them, or appreciate the gift-buying process and the cost entailed in buying the gifts.

I was frazzled and expecting perfect, holiday-enthused kids who would be joyful to help me as I worked excessive hours in a stress-filled job with demands that peaked seasonally between October and January.

How could they not want to help Mom and make this a great family bonding, memory-making season? How could they not appreciate all the money spent on gifts and my thoughtfulness in purchases?

Instead, I would find myself on Christmas morning in a state of distress, sitting behind a local high school in my pajamas, wearing a baseball cap, and crying year after year. This was after sleeplessness, yelling at my boys, and feeling unappreciated for all I had done.

I would also put myself into thousands of dollars of debt between November and December, which would take me until at least June to pay off. This added to the financial pressure and strain I had been under before the holidays.

After three years of observing my traditional holiday meltdown, my good friend, Amy, told me to make a choice—either I stop with the expectations I was putting on myself and everyone else, which was creating stress, *OR* I stop complaining to her. I remember being annoyed with this friend for not empathizing with me about how selfish and unappreciative my kids were. But that third year, after a particularly stressful holiday where I again sat in the back of the high school, I heard her voice echoing in my head and realized she was right. **I was the problem**, and **I needed to change.**

02 *How I Changed My Ways*

Fast-forward to June after that holiday. I had painfully crawled out of debt (again) and decided to make small changes, beginning with how I shopped. I realized that the pattern of debt and high interest rates on my credit card would not work, nor would the stress I created for my family during the holidays.

I started by making a list of who I wanted to buy for and who I could deprioritize.

I started organizing better. I had a yearly pattern of losing gifts and spending well above my means.

I started by making **small changes**.

Where to Begin

Here are the initial steps that I started to take when the pain and stress was fresh in my annual post-holiday misery. I've learned in my mental health and life coaching career that pain can be a strong motivator! Start with simple steps...

• Develop a shopping strategy to buy a few gifts each month

• Create a yearly theme for gift-buying

• Set and maintain a budget and track your purchases by the person's name, the item bought, and the money spent

   ◦ I use a simple Excel spreadsheet saved to a cloud account that I can access from my phone or computer, which allows me to update it at the time of purchase!

• Shop with local artisans and small businesses and look for end-of-year discounts after the holidays

• Start next year's Christmas shopping by taking advantage of post-holiday sales. If you do not celebrate Christmas, this is the time of year you can traditionally find great deals.

• Carry a little spirit of the holidays with you year-round! Keeping gift-giving in the back of your mind not only helps to find that perfect gift for that uncle who is so difficult to buy for, but you get to experience a little holiday magic on a random Tuesday!

We will cover all of this, and I encourage you to pick and choose what tools you think will work. I will share the system I created over several years as it has truly helped me enjoy the holidays. I have less stress, anxiety, debt, and more peace. I can be present during the holidays with my family.

When others are frenzied and frazzled in December, I have hot stone massages and a holiday manicure/pedicure. On top of that, I have become more creative in giving gifts!

Get Organized!

I want to emphasize again that I started by making **small changes**. These steps did not happen overnight.

In the first year, I made a list of who I would buy for and set a budget. In my second year, I created an Excel spreadsheet with a list of who I buy for, gift ideas, and a budget. I also bought things on sale at the end of December/beginning of January to help me spend less. In the third year, I designated dedicated storage bins to keep items I purchased in one place since I would often lose track of what I bought and what I had hidden from my snooping children. In the fourth year, I began shopping using a core theme. Each year, I pick a theme for gift-giving and rotate some of my favorite places to shop. I have had themes using candles, custom hand towels, and socks. Once, I found a floating pen vendor who customized gifts.

I also make gifts for my boys, nephews, and my partner's daughter. They are young adults and want money or gift cards, which makes gift-giving less fun for me. I will share some creative ideas to make this more fun.

How to Shop By Month

The next pages have a monthly checklist as well as an area for notes to capture your own traditions or ideas.

Holiday Gift List
1. Mom
2. Dad
3. Sister
4.
5.

I N DECEMBER, once I have finished wrapping/gift bagging/gift boxing, I make a list of supplies I will need for next year. My list has gift tags, gift wrap, decorative boxes, gift bags, tissue paper, and tape.

I wait to shop for those items until the day after Christmas and head to Walmart and local pharmacies to pick up supplies. I shop for about two hours for unique items to wrap them in, such as metal pails and decorative containers. I also look for marked-down gift items.

I look for sports-themed items and collectibles my family and friends enjoy. I have friends who love hedgehogs, turtles, elephants, and Harry Potter. I try to find fun gifts like socks, hand towels, ornaments, pens, backscratchers, glass nail files, and beauty sponges. I place the items in storage bins. I keep the receipts in a folder.

GIFTS I'VE MADE

For this gift, I bought a mason jar, glued a piece of cardboard as a base, and then glued a toilet paper roll to the base. I rolled money into the toilet paper roll and glued cardboard to the top of the toilet paper roll. I added candy around the roll, bought a Santa ribbon and the person's initial, and glued them to the jar.

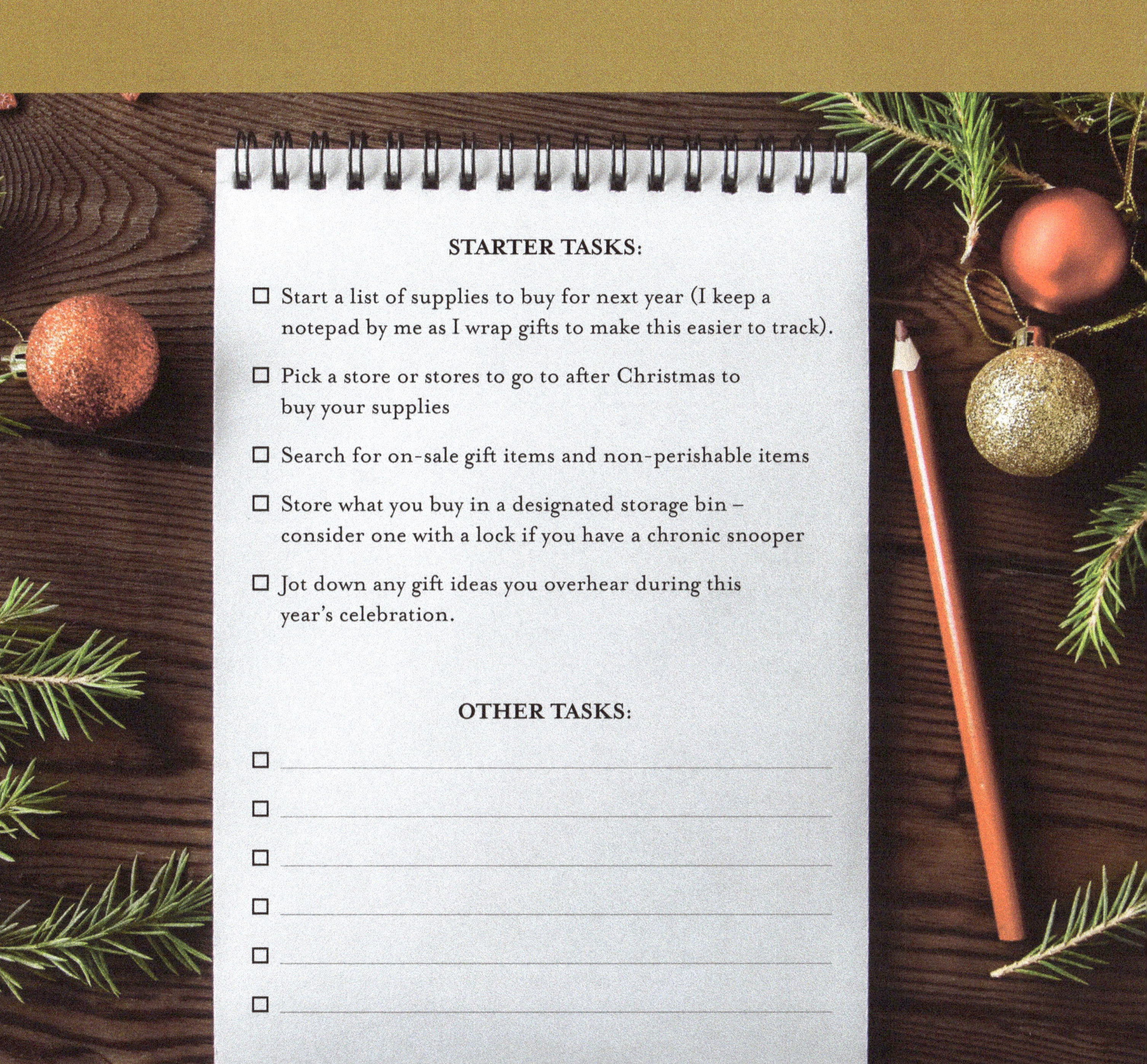

STARTER TASKS:

☐ Start a list of supplies to buy for next year (I keep a
notepad by me as I wrap gifts to make this easier to track).

☐ Pick a store or stores to go to after Christmas to
buy your supplies

☐ Search for on-sale gift items and non-perishable items

☐ Store what you buy in a designated storage bin –
consider one with a lock if you have a chronic snooper

☐ Jot down any gift ideas you overhear during this
year's celebration.

OTHER TASKS:

☐ ____

☐ ____

☐ ____

☐ ____

☐ ____

☐ ____

January

IN JANUARY, I update my holiday list of who I want to buy gifts for and look for items marked down. I will look for hoodies and pajamas, as I give my boys pajamas every Christmas Eve. I also look for sports-themed clothing, ornaments, and any other gift that may be 60% or more off the original price. For clothing, you may want to wait if you have children who are going to grow over the course of the year, in my partner's case, he lost 40 lbs. in a year, and I had custom-made a few t-shirts for him!

I decide on a theme for the season and buy items around the theme. One year, I decided to buy socks. I looked for sports teams, firefighters/police, military, hobbies (golf, fishing, bowling, hedgehogs, and turtles). The purchases were specific to the person I was buying for.

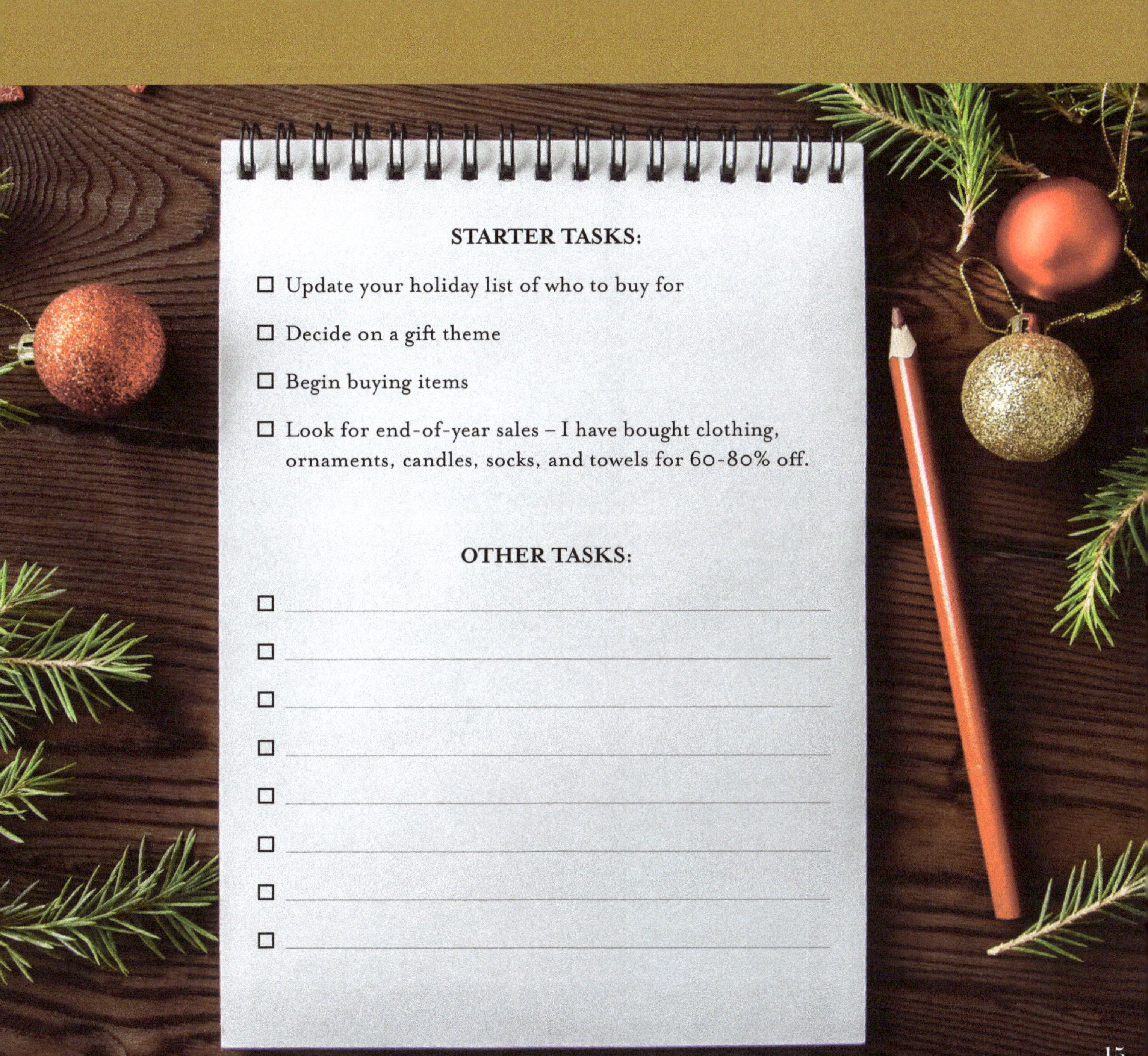

STARTER TASKS:

☐ Update your holiday list of who to buy for

☐ Decide on a gift theme

☐ Begin buying items

☐ Look for end-of-year sales – I have bought clothing,
ornaments, candles, socks, and towels for 60-80% off.

OTHER TASKS:

February

IN FEBRUARY, I casually go to stores to see if I can find further discounted items. By this time, items may be reduced by 80%.

GIFTS I'VE MADE

I saved tissue boxes and toilet paper rolls and then taped 50 $1 bills to make a money chain. I put a Post-it on top with the label, "Don't BLOW it all in one place!" When the gift receiver lifted the label, they pulled the Post-it tab and found a garland of dollars.

STARTER TASKS:
Head to stores to see about additional discounts on items
OTHER TASKS:

March

IN MARCH, I start an Excel spreadsheet for the year and inventory what I have already purchased. I then set my budget for each person. I will note gifts they might like, such as favorite restaurants and shops. Here is a sample of my Excel sheet:

Person	Budget	Person	Budget	Person	Budget
Mom	**100**	**Dad**	**100**	**M**	**100**
Nail Salon	50	Outback Steakhouse	50	49ers Sweats	25
Hair Salon					
L	**100**	**J**	**100**	**K**	**25**
Pottery Bowl		Jets Hoodie		Etsy Gift Certificate	
		Chipotle Giftcard			
Hairdresser		**Teachers**			
Loves Coffee		Scratch-off Lotto			

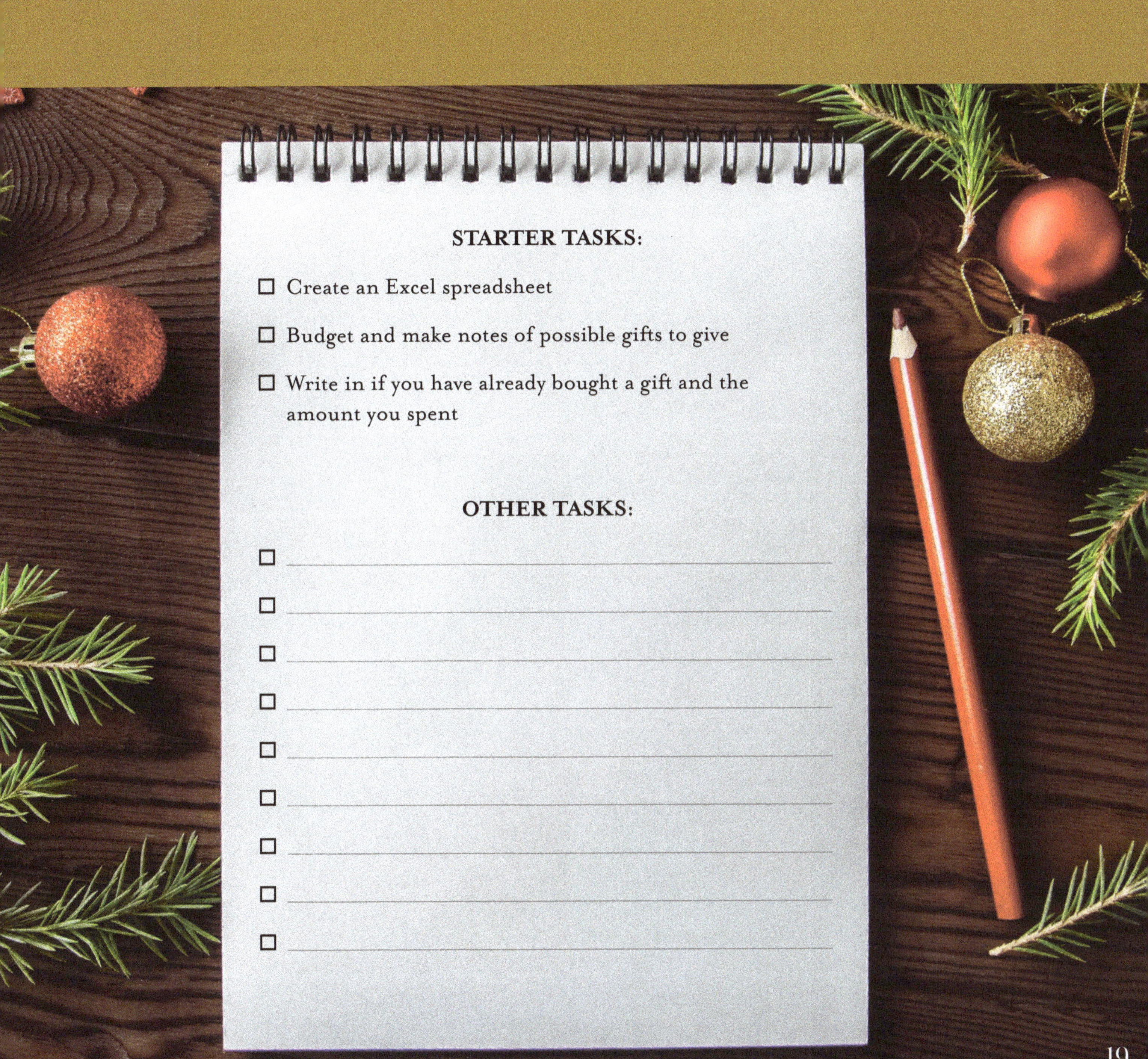

STARTER TASKS:

☐ Create an Excel spreadsheet

☐ Budget and make notes of possible gifts to give

☐ Write in if you have already bought a gift and the
amount you spent

OTHER TASKS:

April

IN APRIL, I plan around my tax return to put the money aside for bigger purchases because I wait for sales in the Fall. If you do not get a tax return, set money aside each month for bigger-ticket items.

I also go to my favorite vendors on Etsy. When I find a vendor I love, I favorite them so that I can easily return to their store. Artisans and small businesses get very busy during the holidays, so — I want to give vendors enough notice to craft items for me.

> Artisans and small businesses get very busy during the holidays, and I want to give vendors enough notice to craft items for me.

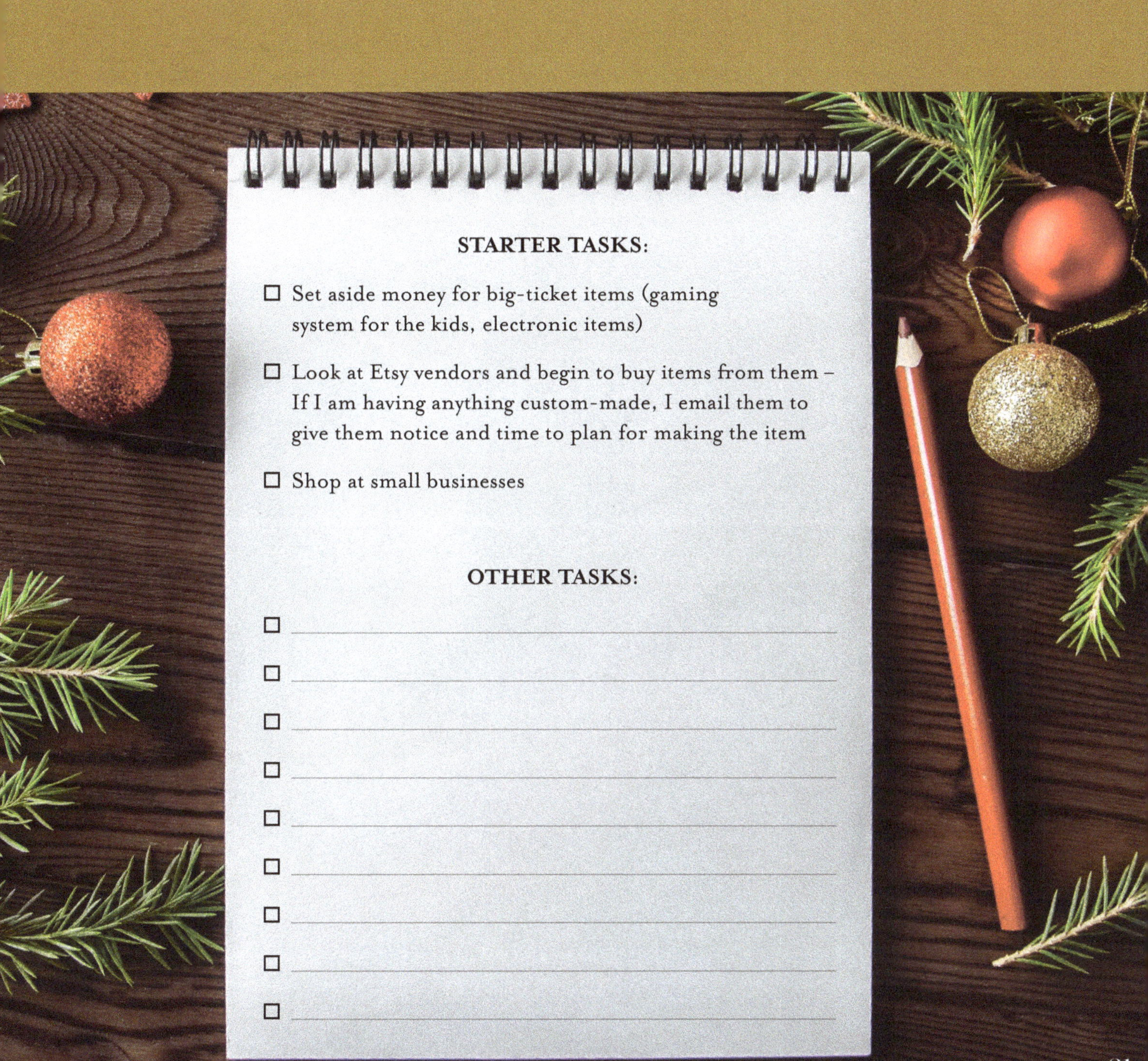

STARTER TASKS:

☐ Set aside money for big-ticket items (gaming system for the kids, electronic items)

☐ Look at Etsy vendors and begin to buy items from them – If I am having anything custom-made, I email them to give them notice and time to plan for making the item

☐ Shop at small businesses

OTHER TASKS:

May

I N MAY, I attend my first craft fair. I love artisans and crafters for unique gift buying, and I support local businesses. I buy soaps, honey, hot sauce, bookmarks, jewelry, and pottery.

GIFTS I'VE MADE

This was a gift I made for my mom. I bought a plain chalkboard with a wood border, painted the border blue, and glued various floral items. I also bought a stand for her to place her gift where she wanted in her house.

STARTER TASKS:

☐ Attend craft fairs in your area or nearby

☐ Buy from small business owners in your community

OTHER TASKS:

June

In June, I finish buying my theme items. I look for summer festivals and fairs. Several towns have street fairs where vendors will be, as well as farmers' markets. You never know what you will find.

GIFTS I'VE MADE

The treasure chest was a fun gift. I put money and scratch-off lotto tickets on the bottom and then added the gold coin chocolates and other gold-wrapped candy.

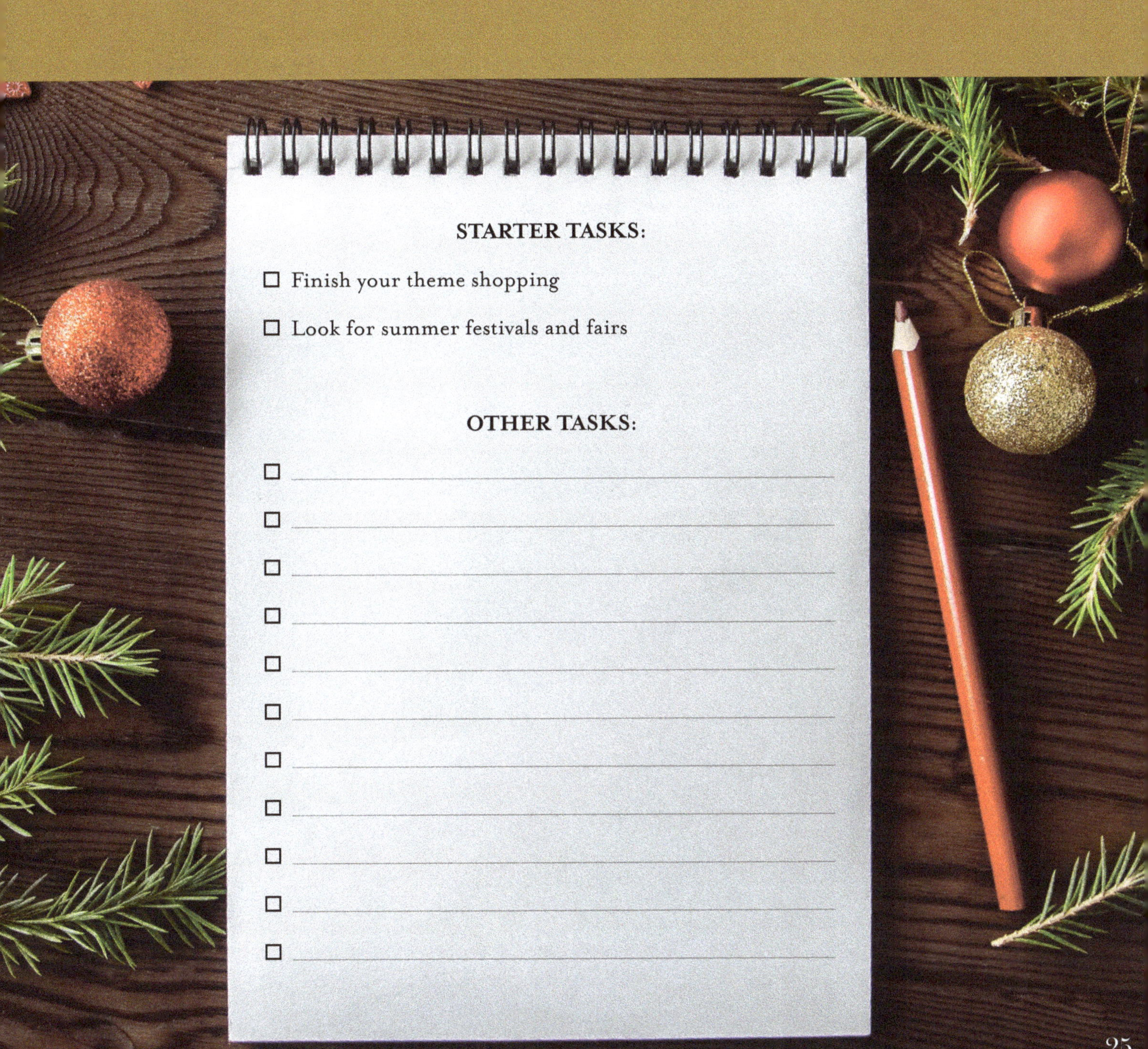

STARTER TASKS:

☐ Finish your theme shopping

☐ Look for summer festivals and fairs

OTHER TASKS:

IN JULY, I attend Christmas in July events and markets.

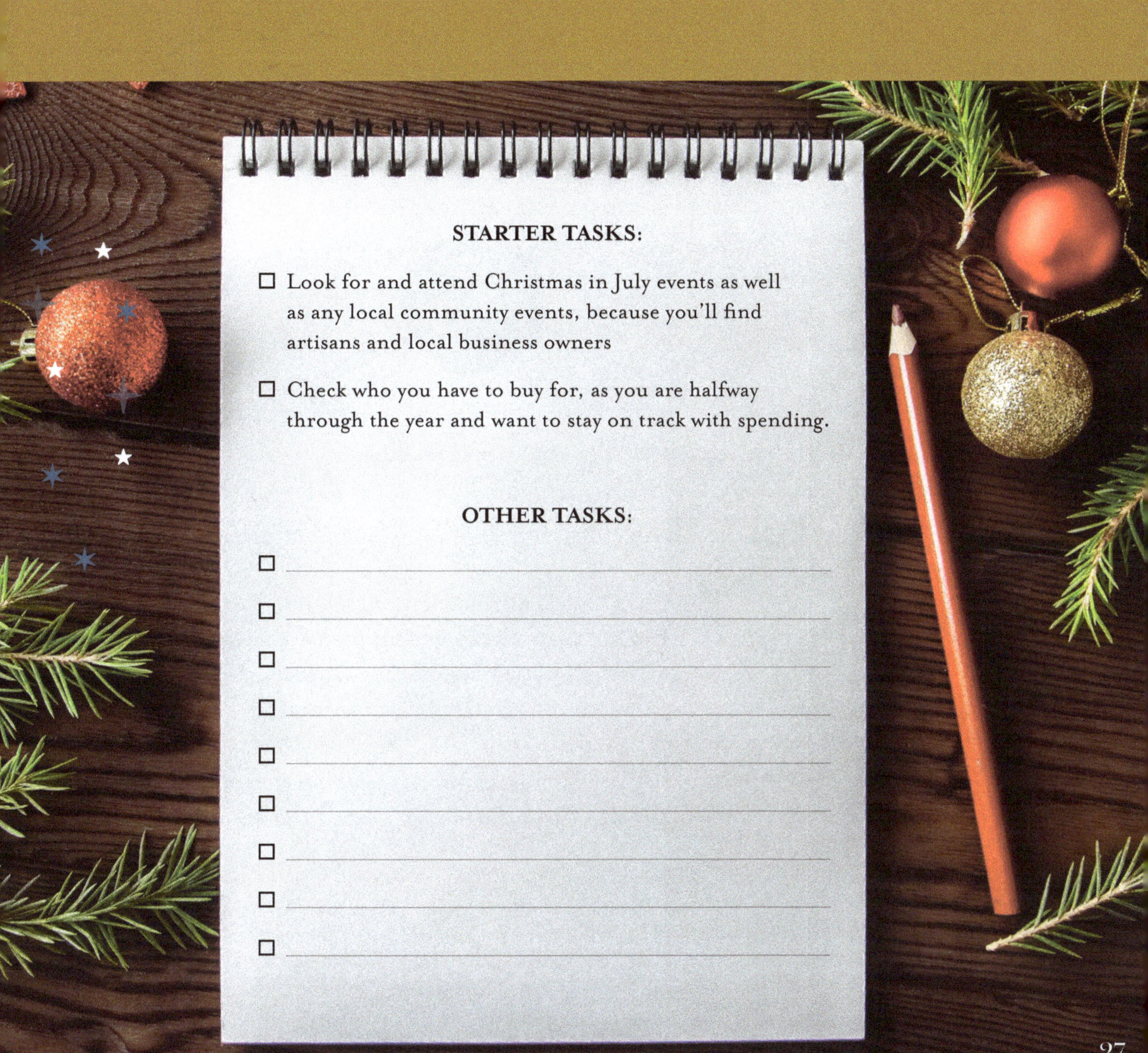

STARTER TASKS:

Look for and attend Christmas in July events as well as any local community events, because you'll find artisans and local business owners

Check who you have to buy for, as you are halfway through the year and want to stay on track with spending.

OTHER TASKS:

GIFTS I'VE MADE

I have a few golf players in my family, and I thought this would be a fun gift. I took a roll of toilet paper, made labels that said, "Because your Golf Game is (poop emoji)," and put the toilet paper in a cellophane bag with a ribbon I tied on the end.

In August, I plan a creative gift for my sons, nephews, and my partner's daughter. I look at Pinterest and Google for ideas, such as creative ways to give money and gift cards. One year, I put money and lotto tickets in pizza boxes labeled "thought you could use a little dough for the holidays."

STARTER TASKS:

☐ Plan creative ways to give gift cards or money

☐ Save ideas on Pinterest

OTHER TASKS:

☐
☐
☐
☐
☐
☐
☐
☐
☐
☐
☐

September

Photo: Okan Akdeniz

IN SEPTEMBER, I head to big box stores, hobby/craft stores, and favorite restaurants to start making the creative gifts. I also attend Labor Day craft fairs

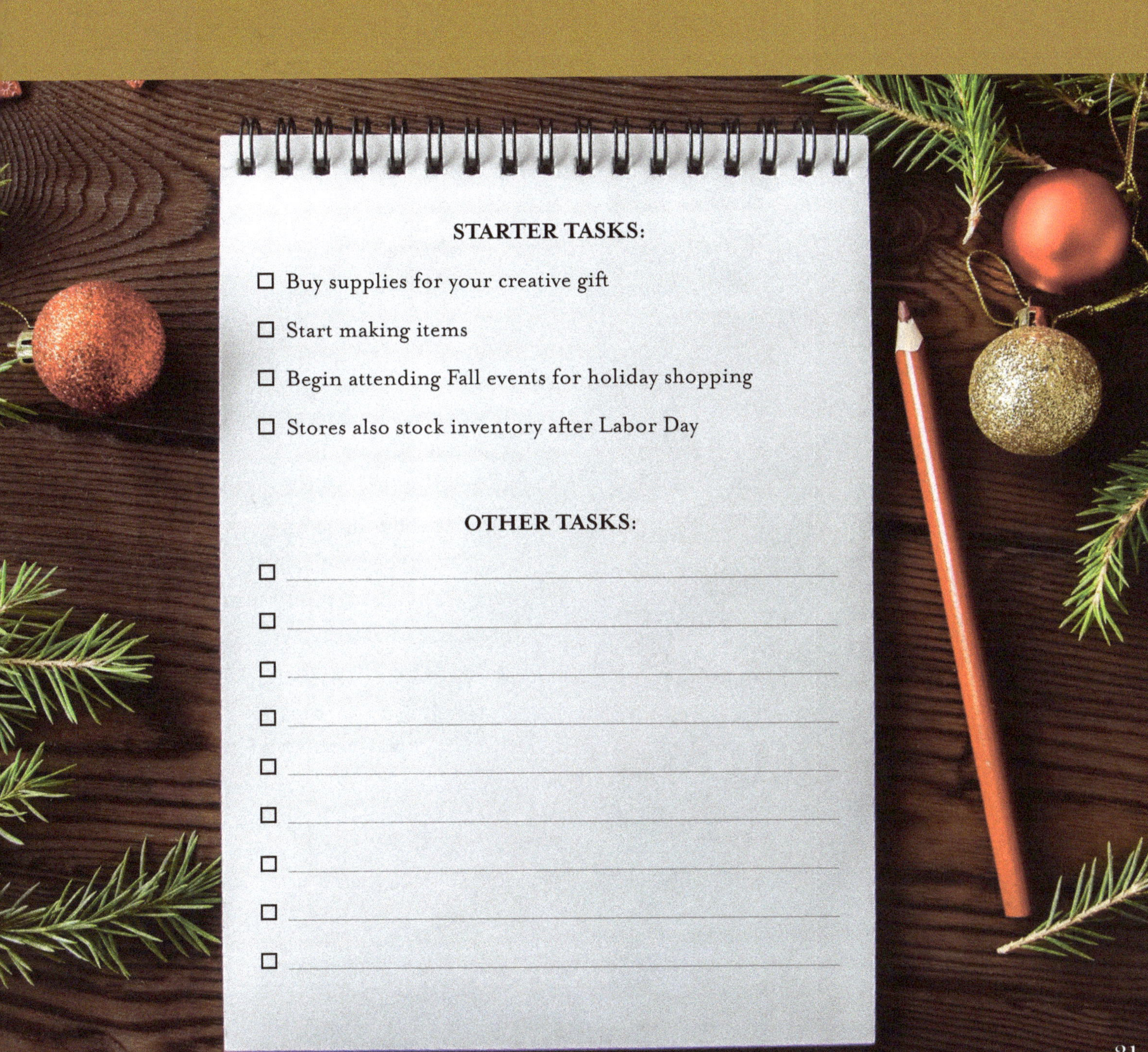

STARTER TASKS:

☐ Buy supplies for your creative gift

☐ Start making items

☐ Begin attending Fall events for holiday shopping

☐ Stores also stock inventory after Labor Day

OTHER TASKS:

October

By October, I have completed 90% of my list. I make a list of small gifts/stocking stuffer items to buy, including candy, wood back scratchers, tire gauges, glass nail files, toothbrushes, and hand sanitizers. I also look at who I have left to shop for and what is left in my budget. I will attend local craft events if I need items.

STARTER TASKS:

☐ Make a list of small gift/stocking stuffer items –
buy some of these items if you haven't already

☐ Evaluate your list and remaining budget

☐ Attend any local craft events and support local businesses

OTHER TASKS:

November

In November, I buy holiday lotto scratch-off tickets as extra items. Buy bigger purchase items with the money saved from April. I then schedule my stress-free December appointments for a manicure, pedicure, hot stone massage, hair color and cut, and other self-care activities that appeal to me. I book in advance since many places get busy in December, and I want to be sure I have my downtime. I then start to decorate the house.

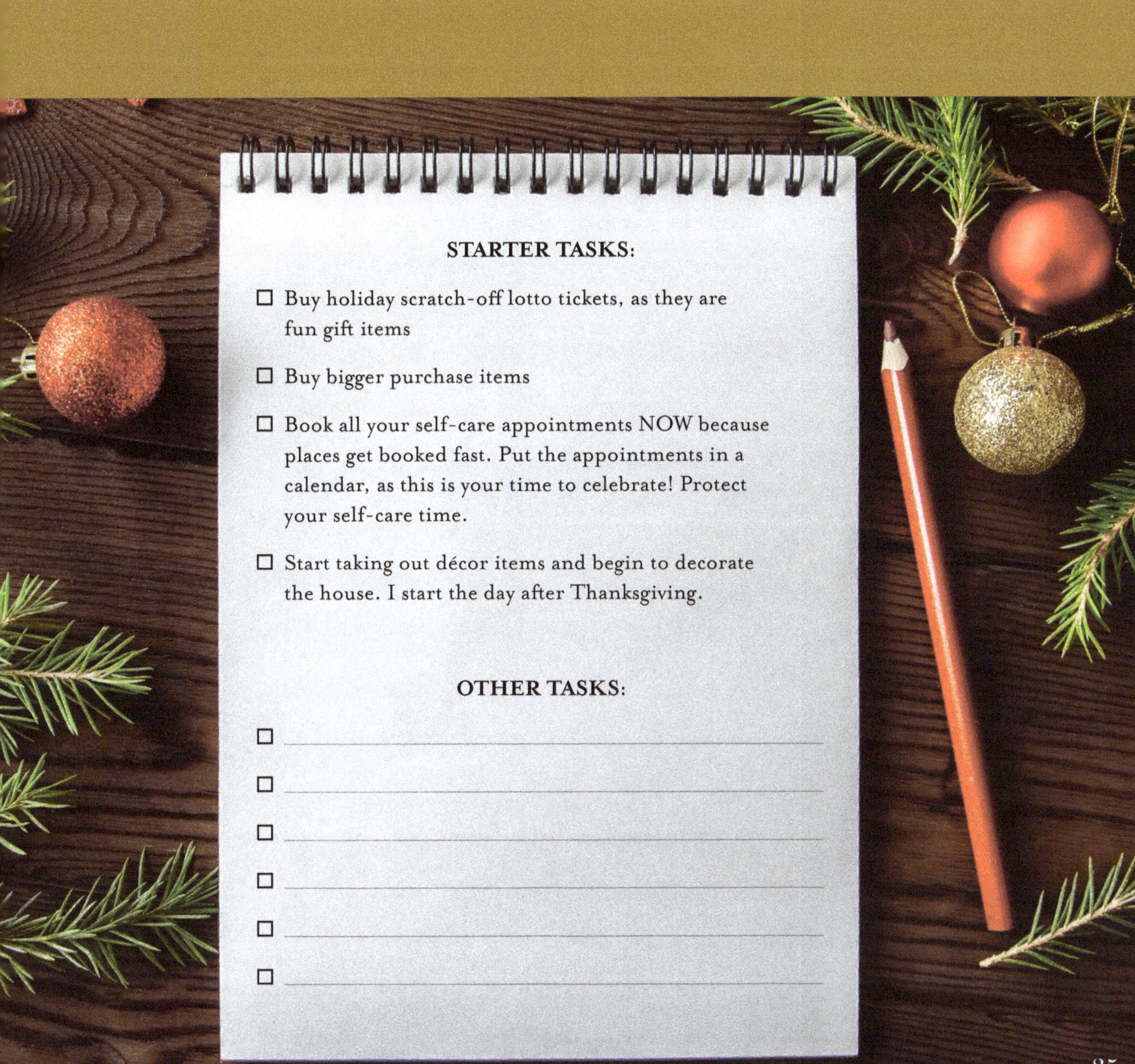

STARTER TASKS:

☐ Buy holiday scratch-off lotto tickets, as they are fun gift items

☐ Buy bigger purchase items

☐ Book all your self-care appointments NOW because places get booked fast. Put the appointments in a calendar, as this is your time to celebrate! Protect your self-care time.

☐ Start taking out décor items and begin to decorate the house. I start the day after Thanksgiving.

OTHER TASKS:

☐ _______________________________________

☐ _______________________________________

☐ _______________________________________

☐ _______________________________________

☐ _______________________________________

☐ _______________________________________

December (Now sit back and enjoy the Holidays!)

In December, I stuff the stockings, gift bags, or decorative boxes by the first week, and I am done! Some years, I attend December craft fairs and visit my favorite local businesses. Most of the time, I stay home and enjoy the rest of December.

Now that you have destressed your holidays, it's time to grab a mug of hot cocoa, sit in front of the fire, binge-watch Hallmark holiday movies, or settle in for a long winter's nap!

> *Grab a mug of hot cocoa, sit in front of the fire, binge-watch Hallmark holiday movies*

Gift Giving Themes

HERE ARE A FEW OF MY GIFT-GIVING THEME IDEAS:

- One year, everyone was given socks. I made a list of who liked what causes (bees, breast cancer, sea turtles), sports fan teams, and hobbies (golf, puzzles, Harry Potter fans).

- Another year, I found a vendor who takes reclaimed wood and makes team sports items and another who makes military/firefighter/law enforcement wooden signs.

- There was a year I found a woman who made floating pens and was able to give everyone themed pens with refillable ink. I customized colors and the floating pen content and bought gift boxes and ink refills from one shop. The vendor even made me a beer and bacon-themed pen for someone on my list.

- I have also bought everyone kitchen and bath towels with their initials or images based on their sports/hobbies/interests, etc.

- I am obsessed with wet bags for travel and bathing suit storage. I found them handmade by a vendor I met at a craft fair. The bags are lined in case hygiene items break, spill, or get wet in your travel bag. I also suggest these bags as gifts for new parents. I remember the stages of wet clothing and endless bibs when my boys were babies.

- I have given photo cutouts as gifts. I had a few made into ornaments to highlight a year of adventures with my boyfriend.

I also have a gift idea file where I keep business cards of crafters and vendors for when I need inspiration.

Etsy.com Etsy also offers the option to create a gift list for any occasion.

My favorite Etsy shops:

etsy.com/shop/AmericanCustomworks
This shop had made items for my family members who are military and law enforcement. The wood craftsmanship is remarkable.

etsy.com/shop/customcutouts
I have given family members and my partner Mike ornament photo cutouts as gifts.

etsy.com/shop/HomeHobbiesArt
"Assorted pens designed and handmade"
This is the shop where I bought the float pens.

etsy.com/shop/KianasCauldron
"All Witchy Desires & Items In One Place"
The jewelry, makeup brushes, and candles are all favorites of mine.

etsy.com/shop/PremierBathBodyCare
"Handcrafted Skin Loving Body Care Products"
I love their soaps and soap savers.

etsy.com/shop/VintageRejuvenations
"Custom handcrafted treasures"
I have bought sports themed items from them and love the quality of the wood and their painting of items. Plus, they use recycled materials.

etsy.com/shop/wetbagsbysarah
"Sarah's Stitches"
I mentioned wet bags earlier as I saw this company at a craft fair and bought items for my sons and nephews. They were in college, and this was a great idea for packing their hygiene items and for when they traveled. I have since had several custom-made bags designed for family and friends.

Other favorite places I shop from:

mexicaliblues.com - a fun shop for boho items including jewelry, clothing for all, home décor and more

solmatesocks.com - This is where I buy my favorite socks and the cause socks I mentioned.

If you don't use Excel, there are also shopping apps. I like an Excel sheet, but if you like an app, use one. I always caution readers to read up on any apps, be cautious of cost, and watch for scams. I am not endorsing any apps, but the articles linked below have additional information and recommendations on shopping apps.

Huffington Post - 10 Apps And Programs You Should Join Before You Start Holiday Shopping
https://www.huffpost.com/entry/apps-save-money-holiday-shopping-saving_l_6378f586e4b0e771d954a630

The Muse - 6 Free Apps to Save on Holiday Shopping
https://www.themuse.com/advice/6-free-apps-to-save-on-holiday-shopping

PCMag - 10 Helpful Apps to Organize Your Holiday Gift Lists
https://www.pcmag.com/picks/helpful-apps-to-organize-your-holiday-gift-lists

- ☐
- ☐
- ☐
- ☐
- ☐
- ☐
- ☐
- ☐
- ☐
- ☐
- ☐
- ☐
- ☐

Practice Excel Table

Person	Budget	Person	Budget	Person	Budget

Holiday
To-Do List

☐

☐

☐

☐

☐

☐

☐

☐

☐

☐

☐

☐

☐